I0143311

All scripture reference from New International Version Bible unless otherwise stated.

ISBN NO. 978-1-943409-78-5

Printed in the United States of America

About the Author

Angie Taylor Reames, author of "Perfect Imperfection- I am who I am" and "There is Purpose in Your Pain", is a native of South Carolina. She has written this book as a guide to prayer for those who are focused on becoming a better version of themselves. Angie finds joy in encouraging others through prayer and positivity. It is often that people will solicit prayers and fail to pray for themselves. This prayer journal will allow the individual to invest in themselves, grow spiritually, and also better their relationship with God. Prayer is powerful and purposeful. Angie wants you to be encouraged in knowing that you have invested in becoming a better version of yourself and it is necessary. Be inspired with information shared that will challenge you to operate in your purpose and coming in contact with who you really are.

Angie is a Licensed Minister, Certified Life Coach, Founder of the Proverbs 31:26 Ministry, LLC, and a Woman of God after God's own heart. Angie aspires to inspire, encouraging others to be the best that they can be. She believes that there are occurrences when one must do a personal interview with themselves so that they can operate at the best of their natural and spiritual ability. Angie loves people. She enjoys family time, laughter, helping people, serving, and ministering to those that need to be loved, appreciated, and desire a sense of understanding. She is known for always having a

A 52 Week Prayer Journal

This is *YOUR* Year!

Prayer Journal and Devotionals

By: Angie Taylor Reames

"Encourage yourself each week to be better than the week before."- Angie Taylor Reames

This book is dedicated to my mother Maggie and my children, Shakaila, Kalen, and Hannah. In my darkest moments, they have been my most valuable players, and I love my team. I thank God for their consistent support, loyalty, dedication, and prayers.

*

In Memory of James Taylor, Jr.
Loving Dad & Grandfather
Your departure increased my prayer life and I will forever make you proud.

Presented To

_____

By

_____

smile on her face and an embrace for anyone. When you see Angie, you will definitely be greeted with a smile and the love of the Lord.

About Proverbs 31:26 Ministry, LLC

The Proverbs 31:26 Ministry, LLC is a ministry founded by Angie Taylor Reames. It is branded by the scripture which promotes wisdom and kindness as this Woman of God has vowed to "Speak with Wisdom" and encourages with "Faithful Instruction on Her Tongue". The Proverbs 31:26 Ministry, LLC was founded in hopes to encourage others to speak positively differently, be kind, use wisdom, show respect, and be the best version of yourself. It is branded to provide clarity, love, and God. Angie encourage women through her transparency and testimony. She embraces with love and confidence in knowing that "God is so intentional", her tag line of ministry. She often ministers from a place of boldness in Christ and unapologetic in her walk with God. This ministry is purposed as an umbrella to many opened doors of spiritual development and spiritual growth. It is a community involvement ministry that pours into those that are in need. The need may be a hug, encouragement, or just genuine love. As Angie promotes wisdom and kindness, she is intentional in her walk with God and the things that He has called her to do.

To learn more about Angie Taylor Reames, please visit www.angiereames.com

The purpose of this book is to enhance your prayer life and provide encouragement so that you can become better than you were the week before. It is my absolute sincerest prayer that this journal will inspire you to find a better version of yourself despite the challenges that you face.

Each day has its different ups, downs, things to be thankful for, highlights, and things we pray for. As well, each day has its own response to the prayers that we have requested. God hears us and He knows. He just wants us to trust Him and communicate with Him. Prayer is a way that we can effectively communicate with God.

In this journal you will receive your weekly verse that is designed for meditation during the week, this will allow you to study the Word of God and apply it to your life daily. It is recommended that you also find different versions of the text to challenge yourself as you dive deeper in the Word of God. During the week you will be able to journal things that you are thankful for, challenges you may face, success plans for the week (prayer and a plan produces purpose). You will also find a prayer request section to add names, things, situations, families, etc., as a reminder of your prayer focus for the week. The great thing about this journal is that you also have a section for answered requests. What does that mean? What prayer requests have God answered for you this week? The requests don't have to come from the week that you are in, but be thankful that they are being answered. Hallelujah! I coin the phrase, "God is so intentional", because He does all things well according to His plans. When we don't understand His plan, He still provides a way that will bless us in season and out of season. Prayer is necessary and purposeful.

Father God, bless the person reading this book. May their prayer life be filled with all things that will enhance their spiritual growth and prayer life. As they grow, develop, and glean from weekly journal entries and devotionals, may their life be better than the week before. May they grow in grace, manifest in mercy, and find purpose in prayer. God, we know you to be intentional, heal those that are broken, make whole those who are weary, comfort those that grieve, love those that hate, and forgive those that have sinned. We love you God. If a request has been omitted, may the reader request prayer as it will serve as their first official prayer on their 52 weeks of prayer journey as they encourage themselves to be better. In Jesus Name we pray. Amen.

Date: _____

This week's verse:

Joshua 1:9

"Haven't I commanded you? Be strong and courageous. Don't be afraid. Don't be dismayed, for Yahweh your God is with you wherever you go."

I am thankful for:

_____

_____

_____

_____

_____

_____

_____

_____

_____

_____

_____

Challenges this week include:

_____

_____

_____

_____

_____

_____

_____

My plan for success this week includes:

_____

_____

_____

_____

_____

_____

_____

_____

Prayer Request:

_____

_____

_____

_____

_____

_____

_____

Answered Requests:

_____

_____

_____

_____

_____

_____

_____

_____

Date: _____

This week's verse:

Lamentations 3:22-23

"It is because of the LORD's loving kindnesses that we are not consumed, because his compassion doesn't fail. They are new every morning; great is your faithfulness."

I am thankful for:

_____

_____

_____

_____

_____

_____

_____

_____

_____

_____

_____

_____

Challenges this week include:

_____

_____

_____

_____

_____

_____

_____

My plan for success this week includes:

_____

_____

_____

_____

_____

_____

_____

_____

Prayer Request:

_____

_____

_____

_____

_____

_____

_____

Answered Requests:

_____

_____

_____

_____

_____

_____

_____

_____

Date: _____

This week's verse:

Psalm 16:8

"I have set the LORD always before me; because he is at my right hand, I shall not be moved."

I am thankful for:

_____

_____

_____

_____

_____

_____

_____

_____

_____

Challenges this week include:

_____

_____

_____

_____

_____

_____

_____

My plan for success this week includes:

_____

_____

_____

_____

_____

_____

_____

_____

Prayer Request:

_____

_____

_____

_____

_____

_____

_____

Answered Requests:

_____

_____

_____

_____

_____

_____

_____

_____

Title: Commonality vs Contentment

Scripture: Ephesians 6:13-17

Thought:

I have found that many people have gotten comfortable with the attacks that occur in life. Many have lost their faith, their fight, and allowed fear to become their friend. Meanwhile, their very life is falling apart right in front of them because instead of recognizing IT for what IT is, they have gotten content in thinking that it should just be this way. When faced with opposition after opposition, attack after trials, tribulation after trauma, and fear after frustration; Does one get content just because it is common? NO! As believers, the God in us should be revealed in our words, actions, and deeds. We should be an example of Christ whether it is seen, heard, or experienced by another individual. But understand that when our light shines in a world filled with so much darkness and hatred, the enemy gets upset. That is why it is important for us as believers to clothe ourselves in the Full Armor of God.

The more we grow in the word and in our relationship with God, the greater the attacks will become. Trust me, I am experiencing it NOW! Some days it feels like the minor things are the worst because they are affecting major parts of my life. For instance, my family, my health, my peace, my career, and/or my mind. However, I am aware that I have to keep the faith and trust God in IT. I have learned that just because the attacks seem common, I will not be content. So, I encourage you that you will not get stuck in THIS place. You will not get comfortable in that place of weariness, abuse, depression, sickness, suicidal thoughts, mental illness, and dark places of life. You are fearfully and wonderfully made, and your light will shine no matter how dark it may get. Light removes the darkness. Be the path of light that leads others to Christ, no matter how rough the attacks get. Be obedient to God even when you don't understand and trust His plan even when you are unaware of the blueprint. The warfare is a tactic of the enemy and his schemes to attack you because what you have is a threat to his plans… But we know that the plans of the Lord for our lives are too important for us to be distracted. Go through it, build your faith, strengthen your mind, grow in your relationship with God and know that you will never be content in Hell just because it seems common.

Closing Prayer: We love you God, not for anything that you have given us but for all the ways that you have loved us. Father God in the Name of Jesus, I pray right now that you will continue to protect us from the attacks of the enemy. God, we know that the weapons of warfare are not of the flesh, but divinely powerful for the destruction of fortresses. We bind up every attack right now in the name of Jesus for we are reminded that no weapon formed against us shall prosper. We thank you for the peace that you provide when we are going through chaos and the calm you give when we feel we are in a storm. We love you and we trust you even in THIS. We love you God and we give your name all the honor and all the glory.

Date: _____

This week's verse:

Psalm 18:1-2

"I love you, O LORD, my strength. The LORD is my rock, my fortress, and my deliverer; my God, my rock, in whom I take refuge; my shield, and the horn of my salvation, my high tower."

I am thankful for:

_____

_____

_____

_____

_____

_____

_____

_____

_____

_____

Challenges this week include:

_____

_____

_____

_____

_____

_____

_____

My plan for success this week includes:

_____

_____

_____

_____

_____

_____

_____

_____

Prayer Request:

_____

_____

_____

_____

_____

_____

_____

_____

Answered Requests:

_____

_____

_____

_____

_____

_____

_____

_____

Date: _____

This week's verse:

Psalm 31:24

"Be strong, and let your heart take courage, all you who hope in Yahweh."

I am thankful for:

_____

_____

_____

_____

_____

_____

_____

_____

_____

_____

Challenges this week include:

_____

_____

_____

_____

_____

_____

_____

My plan for success this week includes:

_____

_____

_____

_____

_____

_____

_____

Prayer Request:

_____

_____

_____

_____

_____

_____

_____

_____

Answered Requests:

_____

_____

_____

_____

_____

_____

_____

_____

_____

Date: _____

This week's verse:

Psalm 37:39

"But the salvation of the righteous is from Yahweh. He is their stronghold in the time of trouble."

I am thankful for:

_____

_____

_____

_____

_____

_____

_____

_____

_____

Challenges this week include:

_____

_____

_____

_____

_____

_____

_____

My plan for success this week includes:

_____

_____

_____

_____

_____

_____

_____

_____

Prayer Request:

_____

_____

_____

_____

_____

_____

_____

Answered Requests:

_____

_____

_____

_____

_____

_____

_____

_____

Date: _____

This week's verse:

Psalm 46:1-3

"God is our refuge and strength, a very present help in
trouble. Therefore, we won't be afraid, though the earth
changes, though the mountains are shaken into the heart
of the seas; though its waters roar and are troubled,
though the mountains tremble with their swelling. Selah."

I am thankful for:

_____

_____

_____

_____

_____

_____

_____

_____

_____

_____

Challenges this week include:

_____

_____

_____

_____

_____

_____

_____

My plan for success this week includes:

_____

_____

_____

_____

_____

_____

_____

Prayer Request:

_____

_____

_____

_____

_____

_____

_____

_____

Answered Requests:

_____

_____

_____

_____

_____

_____

_____

_____

Title: Your Peace is Being Produced from Pain

Scripture: Hebrews 12:11

Thoughts/Story:

I am thinking of moments that I have experienced in my life when I felt like I couldn't get a break. Every experience caused more pain, depression, hurt, and attacks. The bigger the disappointment the more it hurt. The harder the fall the more bruising it caused. In every instance of brokenness, I felt like I was not going to make it through.

As I read the Hebrews 12(NIV), I began thinking of how life will make you feel like you are worth nothing but a struggle. But I am reminded in Hebrews 12:11 that, "No discipline seems pleasant at the time, but painful. Later on, however, it produces a harvest of righteousness and peace for those who have been trained by it." The things that we go through don't feel good but I firmly believe that God doesn't give us anything that we aren't strong enough to handle. Not only that, He gives us everything that we can handle, He disciplines us for our good, in order that we may share in His holiness (Heb 12:10). We love our earthly dads and we respect them; they discipline us the best way that they know how because they love us. In the same way, God disciplines us because He loves us. He gives us the things that will make us better.

So, when it seems like chaos is the norm and even the sunshine that is coming through dark clouds seems like a storm. I encourage you to know and believe that it is in those moments that peace, the fruit of the spirit is being produced from the pain that you are experiencing. If we can have faith that the earthly seeds that we plant in the ground will produce crop. Imagine what will harvest when we allow God to plant seeds that produce peace, love, joy, righteousness, and so much more. A planted seed is nothing more than that, a planted seed. But the God that I serve will allow the pain from the dirt that the world may throw on you to produce a harvest of righteousness and peace. The situation may seem painful but God is only disciplining you to bring you something good. I encourage you to know that your peace is being produced from your pain.

Closing Prayer:

Father God, even now, when I am going through unexpected pain, I will trust you. I believe that you will give me peace that surpasses all understanding. I believe that when I am in pain that it will birth purpose and fruits of the spirit, I will give you the glory. I love you God for loving me and allowing me to have life and live it in You God. I thank you for allowing me to rest in peace and still live. I thank you God for Jesus and I ask that you continue to mold me and strengthen me when I feel weak and burdened. I love you God and I owe you my life, In Jesus Name. Amen.

Date: _____

This week's verse:

Psalm 62:6

"He only is my Rock and my salvation; he is my high tower; I will not be greatly moved."

I am thankful for:

_____

_____

_____

_____

_____

_____

_____

_____

_____

_____

Challenges this week include:

_____

_____

_____

_____

_____

_____

_____

My plan for success this week includes:

_____

_____

_____

_____

_____

_____

_____

_____

Prayer Request:

_____

_____

_____

_____

_____

_____

_____

Answered Requests:

_____

_____

_____

_____

_____

_____

_____

_____

_____

Date: _____

This week's verse:

Psalm 118:14-16

"The Lord is my strength and my song; he has become
my salvation. The sound of joy and salvation is in the
tents of the upright; the right hand of the Lord does
works of power. The right hand of the Lord is lifted up;
the right hand of the Lord does works of power."

I am thankful for:

_____

_____

_____

_____

_____

_____

_____

_____

_____

Challenges this week include:

_____

_____

_____

_____

_____

_____

_____

My plan for success this week includes:

_____

_____

_____

_____

_____

_____

_____

_____

_____

Prayer Request:

_____

_____

_____

_____

_____

_____

_____

_____

Answered Requests:

_____

_____

_____

_____

_____

_____

_____

_____

Date: _____

This week's verse:

Psalm 119:114-115

"You are my secret place and my breastplate against danger; my hope is in your word. Go far from me, you evil-doers; so that I may keep the teachings of my God."

I am thankful for:

_____

_____

_____

_____

_____

_____

_____

_____

_____

_____

_____

_____

Challenges this week include:

_____

_____

_____

_____

_____

_____

_____

My plan for success this week includes:

_____

_____

_____

_____

_____

_____

_____

Prayer Request:

_____

_____

_____

_____

_____

_____

_____

Answered Requests:

_____

_____

_____

_____

_____

_____

_____

_____

Date: _____

This week's verse:

Psalm 138:3

"When my cry came to your ears you gave me an answer, and made me great with strength in my soul."

I am thankful for:

_____

_____

_____

_____

_____

_____

_____

_____

_____

Challenges this week include:

_____

_____

_____

_____

_____

_____

_____

My plan for success this week includes:

_____

_____

_____

_____

_____

_____

_____

_____

Prayer Request:

_____

_____

_____

_____

_____

_____

_____

Answered Requests:

_____

_____

_____

_____

_____

_____

_____

Title: Gift of Life

Scripture: Psalm 139:14

I praise you because I am fearfully and wonderfully made; your works are wonderful; I know that full well.

Thoughts/Story:

Isn't it amazing how we hear the word gift and we automatically think of a nicely wrapped present or perhaps a spiritual gift? It made me think of life! Some get accustomed to waking up daily when truth of the matter is, we are given a gift every single moment we take a breath. We aren't promised that we will wake up each time we go to sleep. So, I find it amazing that God thinks enough of us to wake us up daily as He sees fit, blows breath in our body's, and gives us another chance each day. He does this and owes us nothing, yet He loves us that much. Some get "accustomed" to taking a breath when the truth is, we should be grateful for the breaths that we take. Life is a true gift from God. God is the Creator and Sustainer of all of our lives.

If God so graciously wakes us up daily, why not give Him the praise and honor for the gift of life? We all go through things in life, but I want to remind you that you're fearfully and wonderfully made and God has not forgotten about you. If He's given you the gift of life, then He must think you're a gift to the Kingdom. What are you adding to the Kingdom? What are you holding back from the Kingdom? Each of us have survived tests that turned into testimonies, tears that have turned into testimonies, grief that turned to glory, victims who are now victorious, and mess turned to mercy! Our misery is ministry to someone. What an honor and privilege it is to be God's spokespersons for Life! Life is a precious gift from God!

Don't think less of yourself! Your life is wrapped in grace and mercy, filled with breath, given life because you are fearfully and wonderfully made.

Closing Prayer: Father God, I thank you for the gifts of the spirit, the gift of life, and the sacrifices of Jesus. I thank you for life, breath, and a sound mind. I ask right now that you will continue to build us where we are torn down, heal us where we are sick, broken, weary, and worn. Guide us so that we will be, see, believe and remain confident in knowing that we are fearfully and wonderfully made. Help us to know that we have a place in your Kingdom. You are wonderful Lord; we bless and honor your name!

Psalm 139:14

I praise you because I am fearfully and wonderfully made; your works are wonderful; I know that full well.

Date: _____

This week's verse:

Isaiah 12:2

"See, God is my salvation; I will have faith in the Lord, without fear: for the Lord is my strength and song; and he has become my salvation."

I am thankful for:

_____

_____

_____

_____

_____

_____

_____

_____

_____

_____

_____

Challenges this week include:

_____

_____

_____

_____

_____

_____

_____

My plan for success this week includes:

_____

_____

_____

_____

_____

_____

_____

_____

Prayer Request:

_____

_____

_____

_____

_____

_____

_____

Answered Requests:

_____

_____

_____

_____

_____

_____

_____

_____

Date: _____

This week's verse:

Isaiah 40:31

"But those who are waiting for the Lord will have new strength; they will get wings like eagles: running, they will not be tired, and walking, they will have no weariness."

I am thankful for:

_____

_____

_____

_____

_____

_____

_____

_____

_____

_____

Challenges this week include:

_____

_____

_____

_____

_____

_____

_____

My plan for success this week includes:

_____

_____

_____

_____

_____

_____

_____

_____

Prayer Request:

_____

_____

_____

_____

_____

_____

_____

Answered Requests:

_____

_____

_____

_____

_____

_____

_____

_____

Date: _____

This week's verse:

Isaiah 41:10

"Have no fear, for I am with you; do not be looking about in trouble, for I am your God; I will give you strength, yes, I will be your helper; yes, my true right hand will be your support."

I am thankful for:

_____

_____

_____

_____

_____

_____

_____

_____

Challenges this week include:

_____

_____

_____

_____

_____

_____

_____

My plan for success this week includes:

_____

_____

_____

_____

_____

_____

_____

_____

Prayer Request:

_____

_____

_____

_____

_____

_____

_____

Answered Requests:

_____

_____

_____

_____

_____

_____

_____

Date: _____

This week's verse:

Matthew 11:28

"Come to me, all you who are troubled and weighted down with care, and I will give you rest."

I am thankful for:

_____

_____

_____

_____

_____

_____

_____

_____

_____

_____

Challenges this week include:

_____

_____

_____

_____

_____

_____

_____

My plan for success this week includes:

_____

_____

_____

_____

_____

_____

_____

_____

Prayer Request:

_____

_____

_____

_____

_____

_____

_____

Answered Requests:

_____

_____

_____

_____

_____

_____

_____

_____

Title: Show Up!

Scripture: Luke 13:10-17 On a Sabbath Jesus was teaching in one of the synagogues, [11] and a woman was there who had been crippled by a spirit for eighteen years. She was bent over and could not straighten up at all. [12] When Jesus saw her, he called her forward and said to her, "Woman, you are set free from your infirmity." [13] Then he put his hands on her, and immediately she straightened up and praised God.

[14] Indignant because Jesus had healed on the Sabbath, the synagogue leader said to the people, "There are six days for work. So, come and be healed on those days, not on the Sabbath."

[15] The Lord answered him, "You hypocrites! Doesn't each of you on the Sabbath untie your ox or donkey from the stall and lead it out to give it water? [16] Then should not this woman, a daughter of Abraham, whom Satan has kept bound for eighteen long years, be set free on the Sabbath day from what bound her?"

[17] When he said this, all his opponents were humiliated, but the people were delighted with all the wonderful things he was doing.

Thought:

How often do we find ourselves needing to start over? Moments when we've suffered in a place and are struggling to get out could be painful, dreadful, and leave us feeling stuck. For some, that moment is something that happened last year. Well, I want to encourage you that you don't belong or have to stay in that place. No matter how long IT has been causing you turmoil, it is time for you to Reset, Renew, and Reposition.

This woman in Luke 13 had an evil spirit that made her ill for 18 years. She was bent and couldn't lift herself up. She showed up one day while Jesus was preaching in the Synagogue. Jesus saw her and called her over, "Woman, you're free!" Suddenly, she was standing straight and tall, giving glory to God.

I encourage you to get in the presence of the Lord. Trust Him to move you, heal you, and make you new. Seek Him and give Him glory. The Lord has the power to change your position SUDDENLY! This woman was healed at once from an illness that she suffered with for 18 years. Some of us hold onto things for century's, all because we won't get in the presence of the Lord.

Get in the presence of the Lord and you too, can be Reset, Renewed, and Repositioned! Your future wants to bless you but you're exceeding capacity trying to bring dead weight from your past. Give it to God and let go. Your better is waiting on you to SHOW UP! So, don't stay stuck in what's hurting you!

Closing Prayer:

Father God, we thank you for just being you. We thank you for loving us unconditionally. Right now, I just ask that you protect us from any hurt, harm, and danger. Please continue to lead us into a better future and give us the boldness to get into your presence regardless of what we may face. I ask that you Reset us mentally, renew us spiritually, Reposition us physically and financially. Allow us to be witnesses of your promises and our testimonies to give You glory. In Jesus Name.

Date: _____

This week's verse:

Mark 10:27

"Jesus, looking on them, said, with men it is impossible, but not with God: for all things are possible with God."

I am thankful for:

_____

_____

_____

_____

_____

_____

_____

_____

_____

_____

_____

_____

_____

Challenges this week include:

_____

_____

_____

_____

_____

_____

_____

My plan for success this week includes:

_____

_____

_____

_____

_____

_____

_____

_____

Prayer Request:

_____

_____

_____

_____

_____

_____

_____

Answered Requests:

_____

_____

_____

_____

_____

_____

_____

_____

Date: _____

This week's verse:

2 Corinthians 1:3-4

"Praise be to the God and Father of our Lord Jesus
Christ, the Father of mercies and the God of all comfort;
Who gives us comfort in all our troubles, so that we may
be able to give comfort to others who are in trouble,
through the comfort with which we ourselves are
comforted by God."

I am thankful for:

_____

_____

_____

_____

_____

_____

_____

_____

_____

_____

Challenges this week include:

_____

_____

_____

_____

_____

_____

_____

My plan for success this week includes:

_____

_____

_____

_____

_____

_____

_____

_____

Prayer Request:

_____

_____

_____

_____

_____

_____

_____

Answered Requests:

_____

_____

_____

_____

_____

_____

_____

_____

Date: _____

This week's verse:

1 Thessalonians 5:11

"So then, go on comforting and building up one another, as you have been doing."

I am thankful for:

_____

_____

_____

_____

_____

_____

_____

_____

_____

_____

_____

Challenges this week include:

_____

_____

_____

_____

_____

_____

_____

My plan for success this week includes:

_____

_____

_____

_____

_____

_____

_____

_____

Prayer Request:

_____

_____

_____

_____

_____

_____

_____

Answered Requests:

_____

_____

_____

_____

_____

_____

_____

_____

Date: _____

This week's verse:

Philippians 4:19

"And my God will give you all you have need of from the wealth of his glory in Christ Jesus."

I am thankful for:

_____

_____

_____

_____

_____

_____

_____

_____

_____

_____

Challenges this week include:

_____

_____

_____

_____

_____

_____

_____

My plan for success this week includes:

_____

_____

_____

_____

_____

_____

_____

_____

Prayer Request:

_____

_____

_____

_____

_____

_____

_____

Answered Requests:

_____

_____

_____

_____

_____

_____

_____

_____

Scripture: "The LORD is my strength and my shield. My heart trusts him. I was helped, my heart rejoiced, and I thank him with my song."

Psalms 28:7 CEB

Thought: I am thankful for the things that God has protected me from. I'm thankful for the weapons that were formed but for some reason HE didn't allow them to prosper. It's amazing how we're protected from things that we may not even see. God has a way of loving us in our brokenness and providing grace, mercy, and peace to get us through. I love how HE regulates our minds when we think we're insane and comforts us when we are depressed, grieving, sad, and weary. I praise HIM because HE'S worthy and I owe HIM my life!

I truly believe that the Lord is my strength. There are moments that I've felt like I couldn't get through. Moments when I felt like I was losing my mind after being diagnosed with epilepsy. I was in a state of depression being led blind through an illness that I had no control of. I looked exactly like what I was going through! But the Lord saw fit to keep His promise, and by His stripes I am healed. He's my strength because He allows me to smile through grief and sadness. The Lord is my shield because He protected me from the unseen, the seen, and the very thing that was attacking my mind, for that I'll forever trust Him. He keeps on blessing me over and over again! He helped me and even when I'm going through the struggles of life, I'm reminded of moments like this and I'm forever thankful! All it takes is a thought! Do you have a thought or memory that helps you get through your current situation? The same God that strengthened and shielded you the last time will get you through this time. That's more than enough reason to be thankful. So even in this I'll trust Him and be thankful for all the things that He continues to get me through. I'm thankful to go through knowing and believing that the Lord is my strength and shield.

Closing Prayer: Father God I ask that you watch over us and remind us of your strength when we seem to lose our way. We thank you for loving us, protecting us, and keeping your promises when we may not even deserve it. Thank you for being so good to us. We love you God and know that we are nothing without you. Please continue to guide us and lead us. Thank you for healing our bodies and regulating our minds. Thank you for just being God.

Date: _____

This week's verse:

1 Peter 5:7

"Putting all your troubles on him, for he takes care of you."

I am thankful for:

_____

_____

_____

_____

_____

_____

_____

_____

_____

_____

Challenges this week include:

_____

_____

_____

_____

_____

_____

_____

My plan for success this week includes:

_____

_____

_____

_____

_____

_____

_____

Prayer Request:

_____

_____

_____

_____

_____

_____

_____

Answered Requests:

_____

_____

_____

_____

_____

_____

_____

_____

Date: _____

This week's verse:

Deuteronomy 31:6

"Be strong and take heart, and have no fear of them: for it is the Lord your God who is going with you; he will not take away his help from you."

I am thankful for:

_____

_____

_____

_____

_____

_____

_____

_____

_____

_____

Challenges this week include:

_____

_____

_____

_____

_____

_____

_____

My plan for success this week includes:

_____

_____

_____

_____

_____

_____

_____

Prayer Request:

_____

_____

_____

_____

_____

_____

_____

Answered Requests:

_____

_____

_____

_____

_____

_____

_____

_____

Date: _____

This week's verse:

Nahum 1:7

"The Lord is good, a strong place in the day of trouble; and he has knowledge of those who take him for their safe cover."

I am thankful for:

_____

_____

_____

_____

_____

_____

_____

_____

_____

_____

Challenges this week include:

_____

_____

_____

_____

_____

_____

_____

My plan for success this week includes:

_____

_____

_____

_____

_____

_____

_____

_____

Prayer Request:

_____

_____

_____

_____

_____

_____

_____

Answered Requests:

_____

_____

_____

_____

_____

_____

_____

_____

Date: _____

This week's verse:

Romans 8:28

"And we are conscious that all things are working together for good to those who have love for God, and have been marked out by his purpose."

I am thankful for:

_____

_____

_____

_____

_____

_____

_____

_____

_____

_____

Challenges this week include:

_____

_____

_____

_____

_____

_____

_____

My plan for success this week includes:

_____

_____

_____

_____

_____

_____

_____

Prayer Request:

_____

_____

_____

_____

_____

_____

_____

Answered Requests:

_____

_____

_____

_____

_____

_____

_____

Title: Hello Peace

Scripture: Psalm 29:11- "The LORD gives strength to his people; the LORD blesses his people with peace".

What good are we when we have a smile and no peace?
How about the moments when we are in bondage and unable to be free?
Constantly fighting battles and the pain of life remains on repeat,
For every breakthrough there seems like a breakdown, daily defeat.
Brokenness and weariness that extends day after day,
Hoping and wishing for blessings to come, being told to just pray.
Tears that frequently roll from our face,
Feeling hopeless, losing faith, no signs of mercy, and only remnants of grace.
Where is this peace that is meant to surpass all understanding?

That cry of "I just need you God" from the pits of the soul, now it's commanded.

The songwriter wrote: "Ain't no need in worrying, about what tonight is going to bring, it'll be all over in the morning"

Perhaps you are waiting on your morning to find your piece of peace,
And I know a man that sits high and looks low and won't leave you in disbelief.
Oftentimes our struggles remain constant and on repeat,
Because we haven't been on our face and bowing at HIS feet.
There are many that go through things with little to no faith,
When the God I serve, will never leave you nor forsake you, in none of His ways.
He is a constant help in the times of trouble and protection in the midst of the storm,
Why not trust Him with all you might and allow Him to be your calm?

We look for peace in the people we see instead of the God that we serve,

And when all goes downhill, we invest our time in the world.

But I encourage you, to whomever may be reading this poem,

Seek God and His fullness thereof and you will never go wrong.

It doesn't matter what your situation is, your circumstance or issue,

He will supply ALL of your needs and in your storm still bless you.

You must fully rely on Him, and continue to read THE WORD,

And protect your spiritual ears from the evil you hear and drama you've heard.

It is time to find your peace and that is with God… You are no longer weak,

The LORD gives strength to his people, the LORD blesses his people with peace!

Hello Peace- I trust GOD!

Closing Prayer: Lord, we thank you for your peace, grace, and mercy. I just ask that you cover and protect us mentally, physically, emotionally, and spiritually. I ask that you continue to bless us with strength and peace. May we continue to be obedient to your WILL and serve you for you are worthy to be praised? God when it seems like the storms of life are weighing us down, may we find peace like a river, and may it continue to flow. God, we love you and we thank you for loving us like no one else can. Amen

Date: _____

This week's verse:

Romans 8:31

"What may we say about these things? If God is for us, who is against us?"

I am thankful for:

_____

_____

_____

_____

_____

_____

_____

_____

_____

_____

_____

Challenges this week include:

_____

_____

_____

_____

_____

_____

My plan for success this week includes:

_____

_____

_____

_____

_____

_____

_____

Prayer Request:

_____

_____

_____

_____

_____

_____

_____

Answered Requests:

_____

_____

_____

_____

_____

_____

_____

Date: _____

This week's verse:

Romans 8:38-39

"For I am certain that not death, or life, or angels, or rulers, or things present, or things to come, or powers, Or things on high, or things under the earth, or anything which is made, will be able to come between us and the love of God which is in Christ Jesus our Lord."

I am thankful for:

_____

_____

_____

_____

_____

_____

_____

_____

_____

_____

Challenges this week include:

_____

_____

_____

_____

_____

_____

_____

My plan for success this week includes:

_____

_____

_____

_____

_____

_____

_____

_____

Prayer Request:

_____

_____

_____

_____

_____

_____

_____

Answered Requests:

_____

_____

_____

_____

_____

_____

_____

_____

Date: _____

This week's verse:

Romans 8:38-39

"For I am certain that not death, or life, or angels, or
rulers, or things present, or things to come, or powers, Or
things on high, or things under the earth, or anything
which is made, will be able to come between us and the
love of God which is in Christ Jesus our Lord."

I am thankful for:

_____

_____

_____

_____

_____

_____

_____

_____

_____

_____

Challenges this week include:

_____

_____

_____

_____

_____

_____

My plan for success this week includes:

_____

_____

_____

_____

_____

_____

_____

Prayer Request:

_____

_____

_____

_____

_____

_____

_____

Answered Requests:

_____

_____

_____

_____

_____

_____

_____

Date: _____

This week's verse:

Romans 15:13

"Now may the God of hope make you full of joy and peace through faith, so that all hope may be yours in the power of the Holy Spirit."

I am thankful for:

_____

_____

_____

_____

_____

_____

_____

_____

_____

_____

Challenges this week include:

_____

_____

_____

_____

_____

_____

_____

My plan for success this week includes:

_____

_____

_____

_____

_____

_____

_____

_____

Prayer Request:

_____

_____

_____

_____

_____

_____

_____

Answered Requests:

_____

_____

_____

_____

_____

_____

_____

_____

Date: _____

This week's verse:

1 Corinthians 15:58

"For this cause, my dear brothers, be strong in purpose and unmoved, ever giving yourselves to the work of the Lord, because you are certain that your work is not without effect in the Lord."

I am thankful for:

_____

_____

_____

_____

_____

_____

_____

_____

_____

_____

_____

Challenges this week include:

_____

_____

_____

_____

_____

_____

_____

My plan for success this week includes:

_____

_____

_____

_____

_____

_____

_____

Prayer Request:

_____

_____

_____

_____

_____

_____

_____

Answered Requests:

_____

_____

_____

_____

_____

_____

_____

_____

Title: God Is…

Scripture: Isaiah 41:10

"Do not be afraid- I am with you! I am your God-let nothing terrify you! I will make you strong and help you; I will protect you and save you."

Thought: Years ago, I walked into a different chapter of my life. It was an unexpected chapter that interrupted what was common, comfortable, and flowed "normal" on a daily basis. I found myself waking up to live in a nightmare of migraines, seizures, memory loss, and depression. It was as if my relationship with my family and friends had shifted and I had no idea how to understand it or adapt to it. In all of this, I learned to trust God and not be afraid, but the process was not easy.

During that process, I had to learn to love me all over again. There were days when I felt like I was not good enough, days when I felt like I didn't matter. There were days that I felt like I was out of my everlasting mind. All while trying to maintain sanity and still be a wife, mother, daughter, sister, friend, and most of all a child of God.

The purpose that was birthed out of that pain and process was necessary. God allowed my fear to birth faith, He turned my sorrow into strength and allowed the pressure to push me to the woman of God that I am today. Not only did God protect me but He saved me from myself. I give HIM all the glory and all the praises. God changed the game. See I was looking at life from the comfortable sidelines before the process, but when it was time to get in the game God allowed me to get in and He changed the play. He changed the play, but he protected me, and I never got out. I was made stronger and learned to pray in different positions (prostrate, with my hands lifted, with tears in my eyes). God is the coach, the assistant coach, the referee, God is the game changer and I trust Him to protect and save me! He has healed my body, I no longer have seizures, I am no longer depressed, no more migraines. My memory is restored, and God gets all the praise.

Closing Prayer: God I thank you for restoration. I thank you for using what seemed like a setback to be a comeback where you get the Glory. I am forever thankful that you allowed me the time on the playing field. God, I ask that you continue to strengthen, protect, and help those who are on the field. I pray that they don't give up while going through the painful unexpected things that are thrown in their lives. For those that are going through depression and weariness, thinking they are not good enough, I pray that that you build them where they are torn down, strengthen them where they are weak, and remove the darkness so that they will know that You are the game changer.

Date: _____

This week's verse:

2 Corinthians 4:16-18

"For which cause we do not give way to weariness; but
though our outer man is getting feebler, our inner man is
made new day by day. For our present trouble, which is
only for a short time, is working out for us a much
greater weight of glory; While our minds are not on the
things which are seen, but on the things which are not
seen: for the things which are seen are for a time; but the
things which are not seen are eternal."

I am thankful for:

_____

_____

_____

_____

_____

_____

_____

_____

Challenges this week include:

_____

_____

_____

_____

_____

_____

_____

My plan for success this week includes:

_____

_____

_____

_____

_____

_____

_____

_____

Prayer Request:

_____

_____

_____

_____

_____

_____

_____

Answered Requests:

_____

_____

_____

_____

_____

_____

_____

_____

Date: _____

This week's verse:

Ephesians 3:17-21

"So that Christ may have his place in your hearts through faith; and that you, being rooted and based in love, May have strength to see with all the saints how wide and long and high and deep it is, And to have knowledge of the love of Christ which is outside all knowledge, so that you may be made complete as God himself is complete. Now to him who is able to do in full measure more than all our desires or thoughts, through the power which is working in us, to him be the glory in the church and in Christ Jesus to all generations for ever and ever. So be it."

with strength in my soul."

Isaiah 12:2

I am thankful for:

_____

_____

_____

_____

_____

_____

Challenges this week include:

_____

_____

_____

_____

_____

_____

_____

My plan for success this week includes:

_____

_____

_____

_____

_____

_____

_____

_____

Prayer Request:

_____

_____

_____

_____

_____

_____

_____

Answered Requests:

_____

_____

_____

_____

_____

_____

_____

_____

Date: _____

This week's verse:

1 Peter 2:9-10

"But you are a special people, a holy nation, priests and kings, a people given up completely to God, so that you may make clear the virtues of him who took you out of the dark into the light of heaven. In the past you were not a people, but now you are the people of God; then there was no mercy for you, but now mercy has been given to you."

I am thankful for:

_____

_____

_____

_____

_____

_____

_____

_____

_____

Challenges this week include:

_____

_____

_____

_____

_____

_____

_____

My plan for success this week includes:

_____

_____

_____

_____

_____

_____

_____

Prayer Request:

_____

_____

_____

_____

_____

_____

_____

_____

Answered Requests:

_____

_____

_____

_____

_____

_____

_____

_____

Date: _____

This week's verse:

James 1:2-4

"Let it be all joy to you, my brothers, when you undergo tests of every sort; Because you have the knowledge that the testing of your faith gives you the power of going on in hope; But let this power have its full effect, so that you may be made complete, needing nothing."

I am thankful for:

_____
_____
_____
_____
_____
_____
_____
_____
_____
_____

Challenges this week include:

_____

_____

_____

_____

_____

_____

_____

My plan for success this week includes:

_____

_____

_____

_____

_____

_____

_____

_____

Prayer Request:

_____

_____

_____

_____

_____

_____

_____

Answered Requests:

_____

_____

_____

_____

_____

_____

_____

_____

Title: A Call to Lead

Scripture:

I Peter 5:4 And when the chief Shepherd shall appear, ye shall receive a crown of glory that fadeth not away.

Thought: Some time ago, I traveled by plane on a work trip. While preparing for the trip, I checked off items on my to do list and made sure I had all things completed that needed to be done. I planned for the multiple days that I would be away. However, there were some things that I couldn't prepare for. One of the things that I couldn't wrap my head around as I switched from one plane to another was the fact that I had no control over where I was going. In fact, I had the written plan (Flight itinerary) but had no control over any of it, other than making sure I was where I needed to be at each layover.

The thing is, I never could see where I was going. But I had to trust the pilot who I never saw to get me where "the plan" said I was going. From my seat, I couldn't see what was in front of me, or behind me, but I had to trust that I would get to my destination. The same is so with God. We trust the plan of God, at least we should, even when we don't see Him. I trusted the pilot and never saw his face, but I heard his voice. We trust God even though we don't see Him. He has never led us in the wrong direction and He is consistent in making sure we get where he has planned for us to be (Jeremiah 29:11 says, "I know the plans I have for you…".

Closing Prayer: God is the Chief Shepherd! And if we are to live a godly life, we must understand the importance of following Him. We must also understand the leadership of those called to lead. There are some who are called to lead and have received vision, assignments, and guidance from God. Listen for His voice, even when you don't see His face. Allow the Chief Shepherd to direct your path. The Glory that will be revealed from being obedient to the call, is God. Trust Him to lead!

Prayer:

God, I thank you for who you are. I thank you for never giving up on me when I didn't trust the plan. I thank you building my faith, I am able to trust the process because I know you make no mistakes. I thank you for being the Chief Shepherd and allowing me to follow. I ask that you continue to build us in the areas that we think we need to see instead of trusting your outcome. We love you Lord and thank you for trusting us to be followers and trusting us to lead.

Date: _____

This week's verse:

1 John 3:1-3

"See what great love the Father has given us in naming us the children of God; and such we are. For this reason, the world does not see who we are, because it did not see who he was. My loved ones, now we are children of God, and at present it is not clear what we are to be. We are certain that at his revelation we will be like him; for we will see him as he is. And everyone who has this hope in him makes himself holy, even as he is holy."

I am thankful for:

_____

_____

_____

_____

_____

_____

_____

Challenges this week include:

_____

_____

_____

_____

_____

_____

_____

_____

My plan for success this week includes:

_____

_____

_____

_____

_____

_____

_____

_____

Prayer Request:

_____

_____

_____

_____

_____

_____

_____

Answered Requests:

_____

_____

_____

_____

_____

_____

_____

_____

Date: _____

This week's verse:

1 John 3:22

"And he gives us all our requests, because we keep his laws and do the things which are pleasing in his eyes."

I am thankful for:

_____

_____

_____

_____

_____

_____

_____

_____

_____

_____

_____

_____

Challenges this week include:

_____

_____

_____

_____

_____

_____

_____

My plan for success this week includes:

_____

_____

_____

_____

_____

_____

_____

Prayer Request:

_____

_____

_____

_____

_____

_____

_____

Answered Requests:

_____

_____

_____

_____

_____

_____

_____

_____

Date: _____

This week's verse:

Exodus 15:2

"The Lord is my strength and my strong helper; he has become my salvation: he is my God and I will give him praise; my father's God and I will give him glory."

I am thankful for:

_____

_____

_____

_____

_____

_____

_____

_____

_____

_____

Challenges this week include:

_____

_____

_____

_____

_____

_____

_____

My plan for success this week includes:

_____

_____

_____

_____

_____

_____

_____

_____

Prayer Request:

_____

_____

_____

_____

_____

_____

_____

Answered Requests:

_____

_____

_____

_____

_____

_____

_____

_____

Date: _____

This week's verse:

1 Chronicles 29:12

"Wealth and honor come from you, and you are ruler over all, and in your hand is power and strength; it is in your power to make great, and to give strength to all."

I am thankful for:

_____

_____

_____

_____

_____

_____

_____

_____

_____

_____

_____

_____

Challenges this week include:

_____

_____

_____

_____

_____

_____

_____

My plan for success this week includes:

_____

_____

_____

_____

_____

_____

_____

_____

Prayer Request:

_____

_____

_____

_____

_____

_____

_____

Answered Requests:

_____

_____

_____

_____

_____

_____

_____

_____

Title: Anything worth having is worth sacrificing

Scripture: I Samuel 1:11

11 And she made a vow, saying, "Lord Almighty, if you will only look on your servant's misery and remember me, and not forget your servant but give her a son, then I will give him to the Lord for all the days of his life, and no razor will ever be used on his head."

Thought: As I think back on my childhood and the Mother's Day holiday. I think of how my mom sacrificed so much to make sure we (my siblings) had what we needed. When I was a child, it seemed as if we were supposed to have those things. But as an adult, I realize that my mom made so many sacrifices to make sure we had Thanksgiving dinner, Christmas gifts, birthday gifts, school clothes, and the list goes on. I admire my mom for her strength and faith. Although she could've thrown in the towel many times, she went without so that we would be taken care of. Something went lacking so that we wouldn't be without. I am grateful for my mom.

I've learned to be more appreciative of those things that my mom did for us, for me. I try to teach my children the importance of acknowledging and being thankful for the little things! While many things may look like they come by easy, there are often hard lessons, battles, struggles, and sacrificing that take place. We must not be selfish and become so familiar with daily blessings that we omit sacrifices. Most of us deal with crucial moments in our lives. However, if we remain faithful, trust God, and give thanks we won't get lost in selfishness. Anything worth having is worth sacrificing. I'm grateful that my mom had the strength to fight life so that I didn't have to do without. I'm thankful that my mom was willing to trust God to make a way out of no way. I'm thankful that, she had the faith like Hannah. Many days when she was broken, and dealt with the same issues repeatedly, she still knew that she could and did pray to God. My mom sacrificed and God always blessed her with more than enough.

Hannah sacrificed her son. Anything worth having is worth sacrificing. Many of us are holding onto the very thing that we should be sacrificing. The Lord is ready to bless you but you must be willing to let Him have it. He wants to bless us with more than enough, if you want to have it… Give it to Him!

Closing Prayer: Thank you Lord for the sacrifice of Jesus on the cross. Thank you for my mom. Thank you for allowing me to offer my body as a living sacrifice. Lord, I give you everything. I am nothing without you. I'm aware that anything worth having is worth sacrificing. I give to you the sacrifice of praise and I pray that you pour out your love, forgiveness, and spirit on our sacrifices.

Date: _____

This week's verse:

Nehemiah 8:10

"Then he said to them, Go away now, and take the fat for your food and the sweet for your drink, and send some to him for whom nothing is made ready: for this day is holy to our Lord: and let there be no grief in your hearts; for the joy of the Lord is your strong place."

I am thankful for:

_____

_____

_____

_____

_____

_____

_____

_____

_____

_____

Challenges this week include:

_____

_____

_____

_____

_____

_____

_____

My plan for success this week includes:

_____

_____

_____

_____

_____

_____

_____

Prayer Request:

_____

_____

_____

_____

_____

_____

_____

Answered Requests:

_____

_____

_____

_____

_____

_____

_____

_____

_____

Date: _____

This week's verse:

Habakkuk 3:19

"The Lord God is my strength, and he makes my feet like roes' feet, guiding me on my high places. For the chief music-maker on corded instruments."

I am thankful for:

_____

_____

_____

_____

_____

_____

_____

_____

_____

_____

_____

Challenges this week include:

_____

_____

_____

_____

_____

_____

_____

My plan for success this week includes:

_____

_____

_____

_____

_____

_____

_____

_____

Prayer Request:

_____

_____

_____

_____

_____

_____

_____

Answered Requests:

_____

_____

_____

_____

_____

_____

_____

_____

Date: _____

This week's verse:

Matthew 6:34

"Then have no care for tomorrow: tomorrow will take care of itself. Take the trouble of the day as it comes."

I am thankful for:

_____

_____

_____

_____

_____

_____

_____

_____

_____

_____

_____

_____

Challenges this week include:

_____

_____

_____

_____

_____

_____

_____

My plan for success this week includes:

_____

_____

_____

_____

_____

_____

_____

Prayer Request:

_____

_____

_____

_____

_____

_____

_____

Answered Requests:

_____

_____

_____

_____

_____

_____

_____

_____

Date: _____

This week's verse:

Matthew 19:26

"And Jesus, looking at them, said, with men this is not possible; but with God all things are possible."

I am thankful for:

_____

_____

_____

_____

_____

_____

_____

_____

_____

_____

_____

Challenges this week include:

_____

_____

_____

_____

_____

_____

_____

_____

My plan for success this week includes:

_____

_____

_____

_____

_____

_____

_____

_____

Prayer Request:

_____

_____

_____

_____

_____

_____

_____

Answered Requests:

_____

_____

_____

_____

_____

_____

_____

_____

Title: Amazing Giving

Scripture: The thief cometh not, but for to steal, and to kill, and to destroy: I am come that they might have life, and that they might have it more abundantly. I am the good shepherd: the good shepherd giveth his life for the sheep.

John 10:10-11

Thought: What better way could God show His Love and Amazing Grace then in verse 11? You see Jesus explains satan and His own roles in your life. Satan only comes to steal, kill, and destroy showing no Grace nor Mercy. But Jesus, I say BUT JESUS comes so that we may have life and have it more abundantly!!!! This is nothing short of Grace and MERCY!!! He GAVE HIS OWN LIFE FOR EACH OF US!!! GRACE AND MERCY!!!

If you are only taking and not giving then who are you helping? This is exactly where Grace and Mercy came from and that would be God himself. Before this world was formed God knew He would have to give us a way out of our own way. He knew each of us before we were formed in our mother's womb. As we walk along life's path and we sin and fall short of God's glory He still is there. Without His Grace and Mercy where would we end up but in hell. (The bible says a just man falls seven times.) In our falls of life, how many times has God given to us? The amazing thing is God gives and we don't even know sometimes or at least acknowledge the fact that His Grace and Mercy brought us through. When we sin and God somehow protects us, that's His grace and His Mercy.

We are made in His image so we should be doing things like Jesus, which is Giving. He gave His life for us! What do you give? Or do you take like the devil? Do you show grace and mercy when folks do you wrong on the job, in the car, at the grocery store or in the church to say the least? Are you willing to give your life for Christ? Are you willing to follow Jesus and let the worldly life go? You see, even you have to give up things to reap the reward that Jesus died for!!!! You must give it up!!! Give up the lying, the hating, the gossiping, the placing the blame, the self-pity, the doubt, the hopelessness, the selfishness desires!!!! You got to give God his time in studying His Word, helping others, giving around advice, giving of your time and talents, giving your HEART TO GOD!!! YOU GOT TO GIVE THE SNACK MACHINE SOMETHING IN ORDER TO GET SOMETHING… OR YOU COULD TAKE FROM IT BY JUST SHAKING IT, BREAKING IN IT. ONE IS OF GOD AND THE OTHER IS OF THE DEVIL. REMEMBER CHOOSE YE THIS DAY AND THAT'S EVERYDAY WE WAKE UP WHOM WE WILL SERVE!!! GRACE AND MERCY CAUSES US TO GIVE WHEN IT IS UNCOMFORTABLE!! REMEMBER THIS JESUS GAVE HIS OWN LIFE THAT WE COULD HAVE LIFE AND HAVE IT MORE ABUNDANTLY… That's AMAZING GIVING, That's Grace!

Closing Prayer: Father God, thank you for extending your sweet amazing grace even when we don't deserve it.

Please allow us to examine our hearts so that we may be the best that we can be for God. Protect us from the thieves and allow us to be the light that others see. Thank you for giving your life so that we may live abundantly. We love you and honor you. Thank you for all of your amazing giving, that's grace. In Jesus Name.

Date: _____

This week's verse:

Mark 12:30

"And you are to have love for the Lord your God with all your heart, and with all your soul, and with all your mind, and with all your strength."

I am thankful for:

_____

_____

_____

_____

_____

_____

_____

_____

_____

Challenges this week include:

_____

_____

_____

_____

_____

_____

_____

My plan for success this week includes:

_____

_____

_____

_____

_____

_____

_____

Prayer Request:

_____

_____

_____

_____

_____

_____

_____

_____

Answered Requests:

_____

_____

_____

_____

_____

_____

_____

_____

Date: _____

This week's verse:

"When my cry came to your ears you gave me an answer, and made me great with strength in my soul."

Isaiah 12:2

I am thankful for:

_____

_____

_____

_____

_____

_____

_____

_____

_____

_____

Challenges this week include:

_____

_____

_____

_____

_____

_____

_____

_____

My plan for success this week includes:

_____

_____

_____

_____

_____

_____

_____

_____

Prayer Request:

_____

_____

_____

_____

_____

_____

_____

_____

Answered Requests:

_____

_____

_____

_____

_____

_____

_____

_____

_____

Date: _____

This week's verse:

Acts 1:8

"But you will have power, when the Holy Spirit has come on you; and you will be my witnesses in Jerusalem and all Judaea and Samaria, and to the ends of the earth."

I am thankful for:

_____

_____

_____

_____

_____

_____

_____

_____

_____

_____

_____

Challenges this week include:

_____

_____

_____

_____

_____

_____

_____

My plan for success this week includes:

_____

_____

_____

_____

_____

_____

_____

_____

Prayer Request:

_____

_____

_____

_____

_____

_____

_____

Answered Requests:

_____

_____

_____

_____

_____

_____

_____

_____

_____

Date: _____

This week's verse:

2 Corinthians 4:16

"For which cause we do not give way to weariness; but
though our outer man is getting feebler, our inner man is
made new day by day."

I am thankful for:

_____

_____

_____

_____

_____

_____

_____

_____

_____

_____

Challenges this week include:

_____

_____

_____

_____

_____

_____

_____

My plan for success this week includes:

_____

_____

_____

_____

_____

_____

_____

_____

Prayer Request:

_____

_____

_____

_____

_____

_____

_____

Answered Requests:

_____

_____

_____

_____

_____

_____

_____

_____

Title: The Power of the Tongue

Scripture: Proverbs 18:21a

Death and life are in the power of the tongue, those who love it will eat its fruit.

Thought: All too often we get accustomed to speaking things as we think they are and not speaking what we want them to be. Death and life are in the power of the tongue. We have the power to speak to those things in our lives that are not in line with God and call our lives back to order.

I recently spoke to a young man and I asked him what was wrong after being called over to talk to him. He told me that he had kidney failure. This young man, in his early 20's has been battling a diagnosis made by man for years. He has been fighting kidney failure and informed me that he was also on dialysis. What he didn't know was that he had the power to speak life into that thing that has been attacking him for years. My words to this young man, "You don't have kidney failure, it doesn't have you either, but by His stripes you are already healed, I speak it and I believe it." We get too comfortable with thinking a diagnosis is the final declaration of our lives. You are what you say. After speaking with him a little longer, I asked again, "What is wrong?" This time, he smiled and said, "I'm healed."

I encourage you that you have the power to speak to that mountain that's been standing in your way, and demand it to move. You've the power to speak to that sickness, depression, financial situation, and anything else that's been standing in your way. You shall live and not die, you are victorious, and you're more than a conqueror. Death and life are in the power of the tongue. What are you speaking?

Closing Prayer:

Father God in the name of Jesus, give us the strength to speak with Holy Ghost boldness. Allow us to change the narrative of the story by the power of our tongue. Guide our tongue to speak what's pleasing in your sight and according to your will. We love you Lord and we will continue to proclaim, speak, declare, and decree that you are God and there is no other like you. In Jesus Name.

Date: _____

This week's verse:

2 Corinthians 12:9-10

"And he said to me, my grace is enough for you, for my power is made complete in what is feeble. Most gladly, then, will I take pride in my feeble body, so that the power of Christ may be on me. So, I take pleasure in being feeble, in unkind words, in needs, in cruel attacks, in troubles, on account of Christ: for when I am feeble, then am I strong."

I am thankful for:

_____

_____

_____

_____

_____

_____

_____

_____

_____

Challenges this week include:

_____

_____

_____

_____

_____

_____

_____

My plan for success this week includes:

_____

_____

_____

_____

_____

_____

_____

_____

Prayer Request:

_____

_____

_____

_____

_____

_____

_____

Answered Requests:

_____

_____

_____

_____

_____

_____

_____

_____

Date: _____

This week's verse:

Ephesians 3:16

"That in the wealth of his glory he would make you strong with power through his Spirit in your hearts;"

I am thankful for:

_____

_____

_____

_____

_____

_____

_____

_____

_____

_____

Challenges this week include:

_____

_____

_____

_____

_____

_____

_____

My plan for success this week includes:

_____

_____

_____

_____

_____

_____

_____

_____

Prayer Request:

_____

_____

_____

_____

_____

_____

_____

Answered Requests:

_____

_____

_____

_____

_____

_____

_____

_____

Date: _____

This week's verse:

Ephesians 6:10

"Lastly, be strong in the Lord, and in the strength of his power."

I am thankful for:

_____

_____

_____

_____

_____

_____

_____

_____

_____

_____

Challenges this week include:

_____

_____

_____

_____

_____

_____

_____

My plan for success this week includes:

_____

_____

_____

_____

_____

_____

_____

_____

Prayer Request:

_____

_____

_____

_____

_____

_____

_____

Answered Requests:

_____

_____

_____

_____

_____

_____

_____

_____

Date: _____

This week's verse:

"When my cry came to your ears you gave me an answer,
and made me great with strength in my soul."

Isaiah 12:2

I am thankful for:

_____

_____

_____

_____

_____

_____

_____

_____

_____

_____

Challenges this week include:

_____

_____

_____

_____

_____

_____

_____

My plan for success this week includes:

_____

_____

_____

_____

_____

_____

_____

Prayer Request:

_____

_____

_____

_____

_____

_____

_____

Answered Requests:

_____

_____

_____

_____

_____

_____

_____

_____

Date: _____

This week's verse:

Philippians 4:13

"I am able to do all things through him who gives me strength."

I am thankful for:

_____

_____

_____

_____

_____

_____

_____

_____

_____

_____

_____

Challenges this week include:

_____

_____

_____

_____

_____

_____

_____

My plan for success this week includes:

_____

_____

_____

_____

_____

_____

_____

_____

Prayer Request:

_____

_____

_____

_____

_____

_____

_____

Answered Requests:

_____

_____

_____

_____

_____

_____

_____

_____

Date: _____

This week's verse:

2 Timothy 1:7

"For God did not give us a spirit of fear, but of power and of love and of self-control."

I am thankful for:

_____

_____

_____

_____

_____

_____

_____

_____

_____

_____

Challenges this week include:

_____

_____

_____

_____

_____

_____

_____

My plan for success this week includes:

_____

_____

_____

_____

_____

_____

_____

_____

Prayer Request:

_____

_____

_____

_____

_____

_____

_____

Answered Requests:

_____

_____

_____

_____

_____

_____

_____

_____

Date: _____

This week's verse:

Psalm 121:1-2 I lift up my eyes to the hills. From where
does my help come? My help comes from the
LORD, who made heaven and earth.

I am thankful for:

_____

_____

_____

_____

_____

_____

_____

_____

_____

_____

_____

Challenges this week include:

_____

_____

_____

_____

_____

_____

_____

My plan for success this week includes:

_____

_____

_____

_____

_____

_____

_____

_____

Prayer Request:

_____

_____

_____

_____

_____

_____

_____

Answered Requests:

_____

_____

_____

_____

_____

_____

_____

_____

Date: _____

This week's verse:

1 Thessalonians 5:11 Therefore encourage one another and build each other up, just as in fact you are doing.

I am thankful for:

_____

_____

_____

_____

_____

_____

_____

_____

_____

_____

_____

_____

_____

Challenges this week include:

_____

_____

_____

_____

_____

_____

_____

My plan for success this week includes:

_____

_____

_____

_____

_____

_____

_____

Prayer Request:

_____

_____

_____

_____

_____

_____

_____

Answered Requests:

_____

_____

_____

_____

_____

_____

_____

_____

Date: _____

This week's verse:

Colossians 3:15 And let the peace of Christ rule in your hearts, to which indeed you were called in one body. And be thankful.

I am thankful for:

_____

_____

_____

_____

_____

_____

_____

_____

_____

_____

_____

Challenges this week include:

_____

_____

_____

_____

_____

_____

_____

My plan for success this week includes:

_____

_____

_____

_____

_____

_____

_____

_____

Prayer Request:

_____

_____

_____

_____

_____

_____

_____

Answered Requests:

_____

_____

_____

_____

_____

_____

_____

Father God, I pray that the next 52 weeks are as solid as the previous 52 weeks. Father God, I thank you for the person who has taken this journaling to better as an investment serious. I pray that you will bless their life, their finances, their future, their families, and their continued journey to better. I pray that they are able to encourage others from the growth that they have experience the past 52 weeks and may they continue to trust you to lead and guide them. God, we thank you for better and we thank you for JESUS. We thank you for purpose and for loving us in our broken places. Forgive us for not caring for the temple that you have given us, yet you allow us to wake up with new mercies daily, and for that we say thank you. Your love is everlasting and your promises are purposeful. Thank you for turning our pain to purpose and our tears to testimony. Thank you for loving the perfect imperfect version of who you called to be fearfully and wonderfully made. We love you God and continue to keep us disciplined and mindful that we matter to and an investment to better will only bless us to become everything you have called us to be. In Jesus Name we pray. Amen

Congratulations on being a BETTER YOU! You made the best decision of your life. Not only have you invested in yourself but you have gained better clarity of your purpose and that will allow you to be a blessing to others. Your investment will allow you to deposit greater in to those you are connected to. Great Job.

As you continue to grow, I pray that you will continue to improve, grow, and be purposeful. You matter to me and I am grateful that we have connected on this journal journey. I encourage others to write their story, write their issues (as a method of release), and write their vision. What will you be writing next?

I pray that this journal has blessed you and will be a tool for your life in the years to come. God Blessings to you on your journey to BETTER!

I really do love you,

Angie Taylor Reames

Scripture referenced from New International Version Bible unless otherwise documented.

Other Published Books Written by The
Author:

"Perfect Imperfection- I am who I am"

(Amazon #1 Bestseller)

And

'There is Purpose in Your Pain"

www.angiereames.com

Pure Thoughts Publishing, LLC

www.ingramcontent.com/pod-product-compliance
Lightning Source LLC
LaVergne TN
LVHW041217080426
835508LV00011B/978